JOHN PHILIP SOUSA
LIBRARY J. H. S. 142
BRONX, N. Y.   10466
14530

STAFFORDSHIRE POTTERY FIGURES

John Bedford

WALKER AND COMPANY
NEW YORK

JOHN PHILIP SOUSA
LIBRARY J. H. S. 142
BRONX, N. Y. 10466
14530

© *John Bedford 1964*

All rights reserved. No portion of this work may
be reproduced without permission except for brief
passages for the purposes of review

Library of Congress Catalog Card Number: 65–22128

First published in the United States of America in
1965 by Walker and Company, a division of
Publications Development Corporation

Reprinted 1966
Third Printing 1968

Printed in Great Britain

Contents

Introduction

'We make our pots', runs an old Staffordshire saying, 'of what we potters are . . .' that is to say, clay.

But sometimes pots are not merely of the same material to which we all revert, they actually look like us. In fact there have been times these last 250 years in Staffordshire when Omar Khayyám could very reasonably have asked there his famous question: 'Who is the Potter, pray, and who the Pot?'

The Staffordshire gallery of pottery figures to which this little book offers an introduction, has a range and diversity to be found nowhere else in the world of ceramics. It looks at human beings and animals in every mood—tenderness and the wildest caricature, deep respect and simple sentimentality, humour and naïveté. Not many of these pieces are great works of art, but among them are many great pieces of potting: and one day, when Staffordshire takes a second breath, we may well see the whole thing happen all over again.

Meanwhile the field is still open to new collectors. The earlier wares, of course, make their prices—although one wonders whether even now these reflect real values. The later wares can still be bought for a few pounds: and thanks to pioneer collectors like Mr. Balston, and enlightened professionals like John Hall of South Kensington who have had the courage to deal in uncharted fields, thousands of once unconsidered pieces have been preserved from the scrap-heap and given their place in history.

Here also is the place to express one's gratitude to the staffs of museums like the Victoria and Albert, the British Museum, the City Museum, Stoke-on-Trent, without whose help and great enthusiasm for their jobs even such a small and unimportant book as this could not have been put together.

1. Staffordshire 'Primitives'

To me there are no more delightful things in pottery than the lively, fantastic, and totally endearing little figures and groups made in the first flowering of Staffordshire stoneware and earthenware.

Collectors have not always thought so, and many do not now. A couple of generations ago, most people looked upon them as rough, crude peasant wares, in no way to be compared with the later figures, which tried to copy nature in a more literal way. But as time moves on, so do the ways in which we see things. Today, with our preference for suggestion and witty stylization rather than laboured likenesses, it is possible to reach back over the intervening generations and enjoy the work of these early eighteenth century potters, to appreciate in their work a vitality, an economy of means, and also that sense of gentle caricature which seems to be a natural growth of the English countryside in which they worked. The famous terra-cotta figures of Tanagra have charm and intimacy and grace, the tomb figures of Han China do really seem to perpetuate in themselves the lives of the people whom they accompanied on their long journey in the grave, the glittering porcelains of Dresden and Sèvres show the human figure in every kind of sophisticated attitude and mood. But only in these very earliest Staffordshire figures does the potter really seem to be having the fun of almost literally 'making our wares of what we potters are'.

VILLAGE POTTERS

That they are peasant wares there is no denying. At the time they were made—somewhere around the beginning of the eighteenth century—the district we now know as the Potteries, in North Staffordshire, was a collection of villages —Burslem, Fenton, Longport, Hanley, Shelton, Stoke, and

'*Bell Woman*' *in saltglazed stoneware.* $5\frac{3}{4}$ *ins. high. About 1740?* (Victoria & Albert Museum.)

the rest, where bottle-shaped kilns stood at the end of farm lanes, where the potters milked their cows next door to their 'throwing' sheds. Here families like the Wedgwoods, the Adams, the Turners, later to earn world-wide fame and fortune, had been established for generations, some of them since Elizabethan times.

Traditionally, they had been making the soft earthenware covered with rich brown and yellow glazes which we now call slipwares: the 'Thomas Toft' plates will be well known to readers. But somewhere late in the seventeenth century—some say by the example of the two Dutch brothers Elers, who settled and potted there—they began to try to make a ware which would compete in fineness and durability with the magnificent Chinese and continental porcelains then finding their way into the cabinets of the wealthy and great.

This they did by going farther afield for finer clays, and by firing them to a much higher temperature into what we call stoneware. Not far removed in nature from true porcelain, this product was not easily fusible; it was very tough and was at the same time capable of being worked almost as thinly and translucently as porcelain. The new material was a great triumph, and the Staffordshire men capped it by applying to the ware the saltglaze used by the German potters at Cologne and elsewhere—by throwing salt into the kiln, where it volatilized and settled evenly on the wares. Table wares made at this time, buff or brown, carry delicate reliefs for decoration, and the 'orange-skin' texture given by the glaze is a real delight to the fingers; the ware is quite as pleasurable to handle as porcelain.

From then onwards, English saltglazed stoneware did, in fact, earn a place in the cabinet alongside the Meissen and Sèvres, the Chantilly and the St. Cloud: especially when someone like John (or Robert as some call him) Astbury, or (according to Josiah Wedgwood) Thomas Heath added to the usual mix of Devonshire clay some calcined flint, and so brought the new ware nearer in colour to the porcelains. This was the material used for the first of the saltglazed stoneware figures, which we may now look at in greater detail.

First there are the celebrated so-called 'pew groups'. Here one finds two or three people sitting in what appears to be a high-backed pew or settle. There may be a man and a woman, two men playing flutes or—as in one case—a pair of not very happy looking gentlemen sitting on either side of a large and rather formidable lady. When there are mixed couples they may touch hands affectionately, or sit far apart staring vacuously into the middle distance, the lady playing with a lapdog. In one case the bottle of wine on the seat between them seems to be a necessary comfort, for the couple have clearly long since lost much pleasure in each other's company.

It has always seemed to me to be rather improbable that in church services of that day one took along one's fiddle or oboe and a bottle of wine and joined in the chorus or had one's negro servant hand round a tray of tea. It seems much more likely that these little groups illustrate social junketings of the day, in hall or drawing-room, and that the term 'pew groups' was used of them by some perhaps over-pious nineteenth century collector. On the backs of the settle there may be shields, cut-out hearts, or perhaps huge grotesque masks, rather like those on some of the jugs being made at the time. What these were doing on the backs of pews seems difficult to fathom.

Then there are the 'arbour groups'. Here, lovers under spreading trees either sit apart rather coolly as though they have had a tiff or hold hands and gaze rapturously up into the air.

There is a delightful sense of parody in all these groups, but perhaps the most fascinating thing about them is the way the modelling has been done. No two pieces are alike for they were not made from moulds but built up individually. The potter has simply cut out slices and rolled out

8

(Above left)
Early Staffordshire animals. All save the cow and milkmaid group are attributed to Ralph Wood I (see page 17).
(Victoria & Albert Museum)

(Below left)
Lord Byron. Mid-nineteenth century (see page 48). Sheep with 'bocage', by Ralph Salt, who worked at Hanley from 1812 to 1846 (see page 37). A 'Tallis' group from The Winter's Tale *(see page 61).* (John Hall)

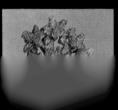

(Above right)
'The Grecian Slave' group by *Obadiah and Martha Sherratt* (see page *38*). *St George and the Dragon* by *Ralph Wood. Before 1785* (see page *17*). *'Tithe Pig'* group, by *Ralph Wood* (see page *17*). (John Hall)

(Below right)
'Astbury' figure of mounted hussar; *'Astbury-Whieldon'* bagpipe player, *Admiral Rodney, and Trumpeter: 'Astbury'* figure of man drinking. (Victoria & Albert Museum)

lengths of clay, manipulating them in the most skilful way. Hair lies in strong coils and fingers in straight lines, like some of the formal decoration of the day. Sometimes one feels when looking at the arms and legs of the figures that the potter has only just finished making handles for a little teapot.

'BELL' WOMEN

Among the most striking of the individual figures are the 'Bell women', for here the sense of stylization is carried to extraordinary lengths. The piece of pottery *is* a bell (or a candle extinguisher) but it is also a woman. The head is a sphere, with bits of white or brown clay for ears, eyes and nose, the cap is a neatly folded pad of clay, like a piece of pastry. The lathe-turned bodice and skirt are exactly right

'Pew Group' in saltglazed stoneware. Astbury type. About 1730? (Victoria & Albert Museum.)

Mounted Hussar in Astbury-Whieldon ware. (British Museum.)

either for the formal decoration of a bell or to suggest the stiff material of dresses worn in that day. This is an admirable example of what has been called 'potter's modelling', that is, something done, not by a sculptor, but by a man who usually makes pots for the table, but sometimes employs his daily skill to have a bit of a joke about his fellow human-beings. The series ranges from total stylization like this to much more completely realized figures.

Perhaps the finest modelling in these early saltglaze figures is to be found in the horsemen, of which we shall have more to say when talking of the earthenware figures to which they are obviously related. There are also portrait busts, figures, and a delightful little race of cats and other animals in what is called agate ware. This is a combination of different coloured clays wedged together, and sometimes very skilful and charming use is made of the colours to suggest markings.

Who made these early figures, and when? Although there are close family resemblances between many of them and also between the forms of decoration used and those on 'useful' wares, they are clearly not all by the same man. In some the heads are like footballs, in others they are much more firmly suggested. The late Mr. W. B. Honey, whose opinions ceramic historians treat with enormous respect, thought they might be the work of Aaron Wood, brother of the first Ralph Wood (see page 17) and father of that Enoch Wood (see page 31) who claimed that Aaron was 'modeller to all the potters in Staffordshire at the latter end of the time that white ware or white stoneware was used'. But as these wares were being made down to the third quarter of the century, 'latter end of the time' surely refers to a much later date than that of the 'primitives' we are now discussing, to a time when wares quite different and much more plastically accomplished were being made.

SALTGLAZE AND STUMPWORK
An interesting suggestion was made about them some years

ago by Mr. T. G. Burn in the *Antique Collector*. He drew attention to their similarity not only to the techniques in the 'Toft' plates already mentioned but also to that of the well-known Stuart 'stumpwork' embroidery, used to frame pictures and mirrors and to decorate jewel caskets and the like. Here the designs are often in high relief, figures of people and animals and birds being padded out in shapes which are indeed very like the stylized figures in saltglaze. Odd spaces were filled up in the most naïve way with birds, flowers, trees and the like in the same spirit. Stumpwork, which seems to have derived from the ecclesiastical embroideries of Renaissance Germany and Italy, was extremely popular in England from about 1625 to the end of the century, and it may well be that we should push some of these figures back in date from the 1720-30 period now commonly awarded them to the beginning of the century—and even earlier—when saltglaze itself was born. If so this

'Butcher's Boy', in the early Staffordshire tradition, but contemporary work modelled by R. Spencer, at the Burslem School of Art. 5¾ ins. high. (Victoria & Albert Museum.)

Bandsmen in Astbury-Whieldon coloured glazes. (City Museum, Stoke-on-Trent.)

would eliminate, as their creator or inspirer, either of the Woods, who were not born until the 'teens of the century. Astbury, whose name has also been used in connection with them, would also have been too young.

So we are left with the not very helpful conclusion that they were the work of some of the anonymous pottercraftsmen who have been with us in all ages and in all countries. That they were made in Staffordshire seems evident by their affinities with the earthenwares now to be described and much more certainly originating from there. One thing is sure: they did not appear spontaneously and suddenly: they must have grown out of something else; and the theory of the stumpwork figures seems a good working hypothesis to go along with for the moment.

In more sympathy with the styles fashionable in the middle of the century, most of them heavily influenced by those of Chinese and continental porcelain, are all the salt-glaze pug-dogs, Chinamen, peacocks, fowls, and domestic animals, such as horses, dogs, and sheep. Here also appear the first of the long and famous line of cow milk jugs, with calf at foot, upturned tail for handle and spout at the mouth. They were apparently taken from the silver ones made by Dutch and London silversmiths. These figures have charm, especially the pert-looking pugs; but they have none of the primitive originality of the early figures.

13

Horseman in saltglazed stoneware, supposed to represent George II.
(Victoria & Albert Museum.)

In its last phase, saltglaze becomes virtually an imitation of porcelain. This period seems to be associated with that of William Littler of Longton Hall who was famous for the very special blue which appears on his porcelain—the only one made in Staffordshire in the early days.

But saltglaze yields greatest satisfaction when used in a broad treatment, not when it is trying to ape the wanton fantasies of rococo Dresden. As Sir Herbert Read has pointed out, each material has its own laws, and once these laws are forgotten it is just as well that the material itself should be set aside.

Cat in solid agate ware. About 1730–40?

COLOURED EARTHENWARE

Alongside the figures in salt-glaze and in many ways closely related to them, are those in coloured earthenwares, following the earlier Staffordshire tradition already mentioned. Here again, one finds the bandsmen, the mounted figures, the 'arbour groups', which we saw in saltglaze, but there are new subjects as well, which we shall notice as we go along.

But first to try to classify these early wares, none of which are marked, most of which show widely differing styles, and several kinds of decorative treatment. They are generally divided into three distinct types, after the potters who may or may not have been responsible for them, but whose names stand as useful labels:

1. The 'Astbury' type. These are figures in white, red or brown clay under a transparent lead glaze. They are quite as delightful in their way as the early saltglaze figures, which some of them strongly resemble. Most often seen are the individual musicians, playing their strange-looking instruments; many of these have long since been collected into bands. The horses and riders are perhaps even better in execution than the saltglaze ones, and seem all to be by the same hand. They owe nothing whatever to foreign influence, and perhaps were inspired by prints or broadsheets. The rich yellowish glaze of lead ore dusted on these figures—both body and glaze were apparently fired in one operation—gives them a fine sensuous charm.

2. The 'Astbury-Whieldon' type. This uses the coloured clays of the 'Astbury' type, but is now splashed with coloured glass. Again the names are purely arbitrary, but since that

of Thomas Whieldon has appeared here for the first time, it will be appropriate to say something about this almost legendary figure in Staffordshire pottery.

Thomas Whieldon started potting about the year 1740, making knife hafts for the Sheffield cutlers and snuffboxes for the Birmingham hardwaremen; he carried these articles to his customers in a basket: and at the end of his life, he had made a fortune, producing most of the outstanding Staffordshire wares of his day. Whieldon was at one time a partner of Josiah Wedgwood and with him produced the famous 'Whieldon-Wedgwood' glazed wares. Early in his career Whieldon started to produce wares in two-coloured clays under a glaze stained with copper manganese or cobalt oxides. Here again one sees the cavalrymen, the grenadiers, musicians, cobblers, singers, dancers, and other figures, and especially some pretty figures of ladies seated in chairs.

3. The 'Whieldon' type. This term describes white clay earthenware figures with the tortoiseshell stained glazes typical of Whieldon's other work, in useful wares. His name also stands, of course, for similar wares made by other potters. The tortoiseshell effect was obtained by blending the lead ore used for glazing with manganese, and from this developed the later multi-coloured wares which are also classed under Whieldon's name. Manganese gives rich madder-brown tones, oxide of iron a warm yellow, and a mixture of these two a darker golden brown, while oxide of copper yields a fine green and cobalt several blues.

These glazes are of a quite extraordinary beauty and richness. They are not all used at once: sometimes one sees only the grey or slate blue on the pale cream ground or maybe just a touch of green at the collar of a figure and of brown or black at his shoes. In style the modelling becomes more considered but it still has the rural charm of the English countryside rather than the sophistications of Europe.

2. The Woods of Burslem

Moving on from the 'primitives' we now come to the full maturity of the Staffordshire pottery figure. It lasted perhaps not more than fifty or sixty years, and has been very largely identified with the history of one particular family of potters.

These were the Woods of Burslem, members of a local milling family. In the first generation there was Ralph Wood I and his brother Aaron. Ralph was born in Burslem in 1715, and at the age of twenty-three married Mary Wedgwood, a member of a family which had been potters since Elizabethan days and which was eventually to produce the most famous of them all, the great Josiah.

Ralph Wood started to make pottery in Burslem about 1754, beginning with the usual saltglaze and 'Whieldon' wares. Gradually he built up an important business in earthenware figures, and so developed his techniques that the early figures produced by him must probably stand as the highwater mark of this art in pottery—as distinct from

One of the delightful animal figures attributed to the Ralph Wood factory; in white earthenware painted with coloured glazes. About 1770. $4\frac{1}{4}$ ins. high. (Victoria & Albert Museum)

porcelain. The distinction should be made for, as we shall see when we come to look at individual pieces, each material has its own qualities, which it is inclined to lose if it tries too slavishly to imitate the others.

There is a strong tradition that Ralph Wood I modelled his own figures, but no real evidence of it. There are 'blocks' or casts used in making ordinary saltglaze wares which bear his initials and various dates between 1749 and 1770, but this may merely be a proof of ownership. In any case there is a world of difference in this later and more sophisticated era between the skills required of the modeller and those of the maker of ordinary wares, however much decoration went into them.

AARON WOOD

What most collectors have assumed is that if Ralph's brother Aaron came too late on the scene to make the earliest of the 'primitives' he may all the same have had a hand in the later 'Astbury-Whieldon' and 'Whieldon' wares, and by a natural transition have passed on to the work associated with his own family. We know that he was apprenticed in 1731 to the Dr. Thomas Wedgwood who originally made the drab-coloured saltglaze wares, and afterwards played a leading part in the development of the white saltglaze

Shepherd with the 'Voyez' look (see page 24), in white earthenware with brown, green, and brownish-grey glazes. Ralph Wood, about 1770/80. 8⅞ ins. high. (Victoria & Albert Museum.)

18

body. We also know that after working for twelve years with Thomas Wedgwood he was with John Mitchell of Burslem for seven years as a modeller and 'block-cutter', that is to say, the man who cut out the moulds from which pieces were cast. This art had not long before been brought to a high degree of skill due to the introduction from France by Ralph Daniel of the plaster of paris mould.

Afterwards Aaron went to work for Whieldon, also for several other potters, including his brother Ralph Wood I. To have created the reputation he did, he must have done a great deal of the better work of his time. His son Enoch said of him that he would cut them in intaglio, i.e. in depth, in alabaster or some such material, after which impressions would be taken in clay and built up into a model which was fired and subsequently used for preparing working moulds from which the actual wares would be made, either by pressing or casting.

It was once customary to attribute to Aaron Wood a great many of the teapots in the form of camels, houses, and ships made in saltglaze, but there seems to be no real evidence to support this. There is a legend that when he worked for Whieldon he locked the door of his room, presumably so that nobody would know the source of his designs. Certainly, from the account of him left by his son Enoch (of whom more later) he seems to have been a highly industrious and lively personality with decidedly Quakerish views. The only signed pieces left by him appear to be a large dish in the Wedgwood Institute at Burslem; but there is also a dish in the Victoria and Albert Museum which, according to an inscription by his son on the back, was modelled by him in about 1760.

The more famous of the models usually attributed to him are the figure called 'Old Age' (see page 25); the 'Vicar and Moses' pulpit group (see page 22); which shows the old gentleman asleep in his pulpit with his clerk reading the sermon; and the mounted figure of 'Hudibras', after Hogarth's engraving of Samuel Butler's character. These three groups, as one might expect from their broad humour,

were immensely popular and made over a long period, as is clear from the different techniques of the examples found.

RALPH WOOD MARKS

But if it is not known precisely who modelled these figures, collectors owe a debt to the Wood factory for being one of the first in Staffordshire to mark their pieces. To judge by the sequence of styles, the earliest seems to be 'R. WOOD' in Roman capitals, followed by *Ra Wood* or *Ra Wood Burslem* in upper and lower case italics; and it has been suggested that these distinguish the reigns of Ralph Wood I and his son Ralph Wood II. But there is no real evidence

TOBY FILLPOT AND HIS FOLLOWERS

(Opposite) *The 'Squire' Toby, in corner chair with churchwarden pipe. Perhaps by Ralph Wood. 11¼ ins. high.*

(Right) *The 'Prince Hal' jug, said to represent the Prince Regent (later George IV) masquerading as Henry VIII at a ball in Brighton Pavilion.*

(Above left) *Martha Gunn, the Brighton bathing woman, who wears the Prince's crest because she dipped him in the sea when he was a baby.*

(Above centre) *The 'standard' Toby— if there is one.*

(Above right) *The 'Bacchus' jug.*

20

for this: and in fact there is a 'Vicar and Moses' group marked R. WOOD with the date 1794—this is well into and in fact near the end of the time of the second Ralph. The firm also had a system of numbering their models so that retailers could record them: according to Falkner, these ran from 1 to 169, but they are not necessarily a guide to sequence of making. There are also some figures marked with a group of trees, a rebus on the family name.

The second generation of Woods was headed by Ralph Wood II who was born in 1748. Upon his father's death in 1772 he continued the business in association with his brother John, but this partnership ended ten years later when John left to start a general potting business at

Two famous groups attributed to the Ralph Woods.
(Left) *'Vicar and Moses'*.
(Opposite) *'The Parson and Clerk'*.

Brownhills: he was murdered in 1797 by a rejected suitor of his daughter. Then, for a time, Ralph II had as partner his cousin Enoch, son of Aaron, who probably modelled for him many of the well-known portrait busts of famous men like Handel, Milton, and Pope; later he went on to found his own business, of which more presently. To complete this account of the direct line, it is sufficient, perhaps, only to mention the shadowy figure of Ralph Wood III, who theoretically succeeded his father in 1795 but died at the age of twenty in 1801.

WOOD STYLES AND TECHNIQUES

It is time to try to sort out the styles and techniques of manufacture used by the Wood family over this period of about half a century; which must always be the chief prop of collectors in this field, and his safeguard against the army of forgers who have been active long enough now for their work to have acquired the patina of age.

To the era of Ralph Wood I most authorities now attribute figures in the Astbury-Whieldon styles—for instance, the always popular musicians. He would sometimes apply a deep brown slip—wet clay thinly applied—to the figures when in the biscuit (or unglazed) state; afterwards covering them with an almost colourless transparent glaze. But his finest achievements are the lovely colour harmonies achieved in figures by mixing metallic oxides in the glaze; blues from cobalt, purple from manganese, green from copper, yellow from iron. Some white musicians and other figures, also some quite delightful animals lightly touched in with these tints must belong to this era, and they are the very stuff of earthenware figure making, owing nothing whatever to porcelain.

Although many of the same moulds were used continuously throughout the reigns of the two Ralphs, figures made after the son took over show important technical changes. First, the firm is now credited with having introduced new colours in the limited palette which could be fired at high temperatures under the glaze—this was one of the reasons why blue, from cobalt, was so extensively used in both pottery and porcelain. These new colours included a brownish and an opaque green, and they were strongly developed by many Staffordshire potters, especially Felix Pratt of Fenton, from whom this type of pottery gets its name 'Prattware' (see page 34). The colours appear on the well-known plaques of milkmaids and cows, on the jugs commemorating Admiral Vernon of Portobello fame, and on many other subjects.

Another innovation, which changed the whole character of the Wood productions— many connoisseurs believe for the worse—was the use of bright colours over the glaze. This required another firing to fix the colours, the result being more brilliant, but totally without the haphazard charm of the earlier work. Nevertheless, the new technique proved immensely popular with a public which envied richer people their Chelsea – Derby or Sèvres

23

porcelain and wanted something as like it as possible in the far cheaper Staffordshire earthenware.

JEAN VOYEZ

As Ralph Wood I had his Aaron Wood for modeller—or so we generally assume—Ralph Wood II had his Jean Voyez —or so we also assume on not much more reliable grounds.

Voyez is one of those oddities who bob up in all kinds of places in Staffordshire pottery history, and a great deal has been written about him—on what now appears to be very slender evidence. He was a Frenchman, trained in engraving and carving, who first turned up in this country in the 1760s, when he seems to have been associated with the sculptor Joseph Wilson, whose monument to General Wolfe stands in Westminster Abbey. He exhibited work in carved stone and wax, and about the year 1768 was 'discovered' by Josiah Wedgwood, who was always looking around for talented people to work on his new ceramic discoveries at Etruria.

'I have hired a Modeler for three years,' he wrote to his partner Bentley, 'the best I am told in London. He served his time with a silversmith, has worked several years at a China works, has been two or three years carving in wood and marble for Mr. Adam the famous Architect, is a perfect Master of the Antique style in ornaments, vases, Etc., & works with equal facility in Clay, wax, wood, Metal, or Stone.'

At first all went well with the association between the thriving master potter and his new 'Modeler'. Wedgwood advanced him money and offered him hospitality in his own house until he could be settled in the more fashionable part of Burslem. What followed might have been foreseen in a note wherein Voyez said: 'If it suits you to send me a Stone bottle full of good porter . . . you cannot oblige me more, for I am just dead for want of it.' But for the time being Voyez showed himself capable of doing excellent work for Wedgwood, and a good deal of it has survived.

Then one day—according to a letter written a century or more later, largely on hearsay, by Dr. J. A. Goodchild to Frank Falkner, author of *The Wood Family of Burslem*—Wedgwood went into Voyez' modelling shop and found the artist 'somewhat in liquour, and modelling a semi-nude portrait figure from a girl who was, I think, the daughter of his own coachman. Wedgwood lost his temper at such scandalous conduct during working hours, and set forth that a workman at 35s a week had not the right to drink London porter, or waste his time on obscene nudities, when he ought to be studying classics and other designs, in order that a Master Vase might be produced by the firm. Voyez retorted that Wedgwood knew nothing about Master Vases, and that it was not study of Italian drawings, but of Nature that produced them.'

What has puzzled posterity is that, as the result of it, the modeller was sentenced at the Assizes to be whipped with the cat-o'nine tails and to serve three months in gaol. Even in days when it was not very difficult for magnates to work off their private grudges with the help of the judiciary, this

'Old Age', by Ralph Wood and 'Girl with a marmot in her box'. White earthenware with coloured glazes. Copied (perhaps by Jean Voyez) from a Lunéville biscuit original by Paul Louis Cufflé.

'Winter' and 'Spring', from a set of the Seasons made by Henry Neale, Hanley, about 1780. 'Spring' is marked 'Neale and Co.' impressed. 5¼ ins. high. (Victoria & Albert Museum.)

seems a severe sentence, and most people have concluded that the incident ended in violence.

But Mr. R. J. Charleston, of the Victoria and Albert Museum, in a characteristically thorough piece of research read before the English Ceramic Circle in 1960, has discovered in the Crown Book of Oxford that Voyez was sentenced to seven years' transportation for stealing moulds and models from Wedgwood. This seems later to have been commuted, which tallies with points made in Wedgwood's own letters.

So it seems that Wedgwood's apparently vindictive attitude towards Voyez after this event did not arise from outraged puritanical feelings, as is generally supposed, but from the natural prudence of a businessman in getting rid of an employee who was a proven thief, and also the fear that Voyez might go over to his competitors and do him financial harm. At one time he suggested to his partner that they continue to pay Voyez for the time he was still engaged to them, on condition that he left Staffordshire. Voyez, of course, did exactly what Wedgwood had anticipated. Once out of prison he joined Humphrey Palmer of Hanley, who was in discreet competition with Wedgwood, and later worked on his own account, making the same sort of cameos and medallions he had done for Wedgwood.

'FAIR HEBE'

Then, in 1788, Voyez modelled the famous 'Fair Hebe' jug. This jug, in 'rustic' style, in the form of a tree-trunk with a spreading base, shows in relief the figures of a youth and a girl, who is being offered a nest full of eggs. On a paper stuck on the tree-trunk appears the word 'Fair Hebe': while on the other side of the jug is a man holding a glass above which are the words 'A Bumper'. The jug sometimes bears the signature 'Voyez 1788', but also appears in some versions without it.

It is generally supposed that Voyez modelled this jug for Ralph Wood II; and since there are clear similarities between the styles of the figures and those of known Wood products, it has also been conjectured that Voyez was responsible for a good many of those made by the firm at about that time. The style—whoever is responsible for it—is unmistakable. The features have puffy eyes, flat noses, and a rather sentimental inclination of the head: they also show great skill in modelling and using glaze effects—nothing whatever like the rather flat work of other artists of the time.

But here again, Mr. Charleston has questioned a legend. He points out that there is no authenticated example of Voyez' work in anything other than bas-relief—like the 'Fair Hebe' jug—except for the handles of a black basaltes vase in the Holbourne of Menstrie Museum at Bath: and

27

Cottage and figures in 'Prattware' colours. (Victoria & Albert Museum.)

these bear no resemblance to the Ralph Wood figures which Voyez is supposed to have modelled. It seems not impossible therefore, that instead of Voyez' having set the style for these figures with 'puffy eyes' he was himself, when he did the 'Fair Hebe' jug, following—perhaps to order—a style already set by some modeller or modellers.

TOBY FILLPOT

Another great achievement of the Woods in figure-making was the famous Toby jug. To keep abreast of technical developments something ought to be said about it at this stage.

The idea of a jug in the form of a figure goes a very long way back into ceramic history, even to Ancient Egypt. But there were predecessors of the Toby in England in the early eighteenth century. They are in the Astbury-Whieldon styles, and they show fiddlers, midshipmen or soldiers sitting on boxes or plinths, in just the same way as the Toby: they also have the same three-cornered hats with detachable cups. About twenty of these are known, but none of them have the slightest hint of the later Toby.

Then, in the year 1761, there appeared an engraving of a character called Toby Fillpot, after a design by Robert Dighton. It is generally supposed to have been based on a well-known Yorkshire toper called Harry Elwes, recording his feat of drinking 2,000 gallons of beer from a silver tankard without taking any food. It was accompanied by a poem called *The Metamorphosis*, or *Toby Reduc'd.*, which had

28

been translated from the Italian of Geronimo Amalteo by a Rev. Francis Fawkes, who in his more recondite moments also offered the English public translations of Theocritus and Anacreon. The verses go as follows:

> *Dear Tom, this brown Jug that now foams with mild Ale,*
> *In which I will drink to sweet Nan of the Vale,*
> *Was once Toby Fillpot, a thirsty old Soul,*
> *As e'er drank a Bottle or fathom'd a Bowl.*
> *In boozing about 'twas his praise to excel,*
> *And among Jolly Topers he bore off the Bell.*
>
> *It chanc'd as in Dog-days he sat at his Ease,*
> *In his Flow'r woven Arbour as gay as you please,*
> *With a Friend and a Pipe, puffing Sorrow away,*
> *And with honest old Stingo was soaking his Clay,*
> *His breath Doors of life on a sudden were shut*
> *And he died full as big as a Dorchester Butt.*

Two ladies in 'Prattware' colours. Early nineteenth century. 4 ins. high.
(Victoria & Albert Museum.)

His body, when long in the ground it had lain,
And time into Clay had resolv'd it again
A potter found out in its Covert so snug
And with part of fat Toby he form'd this brown Jug
Now sacred to Friendship and Mirth and Mild Ale,
So here's to my lovely sweet Nan of the Vale.

The Woods are generally credited with being the first among the many Staffordshire potters who have exploited the Toby Fillpot theme down the ages, the earlier of them appearing in the last ten years of the reign of Ralph I. Conventionally, the model shows a fat old man with coarse features looking not at all jovial, and with lank hair. He wears a full-skirted coat which covers whatever he is sitting on—a chair, barrel, etc.—and he holds a foaming jug of ale.

There are almost literally hundreds of variations on this standard model, to say nothing of all those wherein the original Toby has been exchanged for a totally different character. Among these early models are the ever-popular Squire Toby, sitting in his corner chair, churchwarden pipe in hand; the Shield Toby, with a cartouche inscribed 'It is all out, then fill it again'. 'The Nightwatchman' shows a man with his hat and a lantern on his lap. 'The Snufftaker' is one of several standing figures, another is the 'Hearty-Good-Fellow'. 'The Welshman' has a goat crouching at his feet, and is supposed to be a representation of Sir Williams Watkins Wynne, a public figure of the day; the Drunken (or Unfrocked) Parson shows him in a coloured coat—not clerical black.

A convict, a publican, an old English gentleman, and a royal bargeman all appear, and as in all pottery of the time, there are many naval figures. Admiral Lord Howe commemorates the resounding defeat of the French fleet on 1 June 1794, and there are also sailors sitting on sea chests labelled 'dollars'. There are even female Tobies: the first shows a famous Brighton character, Martha Gunn, a bathing attendant who is said to have given the infant Prince of Wales his first dip in the sea. To mark this she wears the

Prince of Wales's feathers in her hat. A variant of this is the Gin Woman, a grim-looking figure with heavy moustaches.

The so-called 'Voyez' look appears on the faces of many of these Tobies, and some of them are inscribed with the initial 'V'—notably the rare Prince Hal jug.

The techniques of making these jugs, as might be expected, follow those of the figures. They were built up from moulds in two main parts, and the seam joining them can be seen running from top to bottom. All the other parts—legs, arms, handle, pipes, and other items—were made separately either by casting or hand modelling and assembled while the pieces were still plastic. This was then touched up by hand, which accounts for the many differences between jugs even when they were taken from the same moulds. The first glazes used were the attractive transparent ones already mentioned; then followed the 'Prattware' high-temperature, underglaze colours; also the bright, but heavy overglaze enamels developed in the 1780s. Other subjects treated in Toby form we shall be referring to later: in the meantime it seems best to follow the general development of Staffordshire figures by now coming to that Enoch Wood who has already been mentioned as in the second generation of the family.

ENOCH WOOD

No greater contrast with the early figures of the Woods could be found than in those of cousin Enoch. One of the reasons for this was his early training. Sir Herbert Read has pointed out that as an artist 'he was early damned' by being sent to Liverpool at

'Dandies' in 'Prattware' colours.

14530

JOHN PHILIP SOUSA
LIBRARY J. H. S. 142
BRONX, N. Y. 10466

31

the age of eleven to learn drawing and anatomy from his uncle William Caddick, a well-known portrait painter. Apprenticed first to Josiah Wedgwood and afterwards to Henry Palmer of Hanley he set up on his own as a master potter at the age of twenty-four.

He had undoubted technical skill in potting and made some spectacular pieces even in his teens. In 1790 he took into partnership James Caldwell of Linley Wood, thus founding the firm of Wood & Caldwell, which lasted for twenty-eight years. After this Enoch took his sons into the business and as Enoch Wood & Sons the firm traded until 1846—six years after the death of Enoch, who bore the title 'Father of the Potteries'.

The firm of Wood & Caldwell was a big producer of all kinds of pottery, but Enoch Wood's own best work is said to have been the portrait busts and other modelling carried out by him in his early days, either for his cousin or during the period when he worked on his own. His bust of Wesley, taken from the life in 1781, is famous, and he made figures very large in size, such as the 'Mother and Child' and 'Fortitude' in the Victoria and Albert Museum, the latter being 23 ins. high. Some of these figures are impressed with the mark 'Wedgwood' and they are believed to have been ordered from Etruria by Josiah Wedgwood and his successors to fulfil orders.

Enoch Wood had a fine touch in getting a likeness, but his work lacks style. The bright enamel colours he used in slavish imitation of Derby porcelain take us even further away from the felicity of the earlier Wood family productions than those later ones using the same techniques which were put out by Ralph Wood II.

Before passing on to the later schools of figure makers it may be worth while looking back over the styles and subjects of the Wood family and their contemporaries—for of course many other potters followed their examples and even their models.

More acceptable enamel-painted work at this time was done by Neale of Hanley, whose work is in the Wood tradition but has quite distinctive qualities. James Neale was not a potter, but one of those several warehousemen or London agents who started at the selling end of the pottery business and eventually found themselves manufacturing. In Neale's case he found himself principal creditor to Humphrey Palmer of Hanley when that fine potter—who could even frighten the great Josiah—found himself in difficulties to the tune of £10,000. He took over Palmer's business and imposed his own name upon it.

Neale's figures, as has been noted by Mr. Haggar, seem to take us into the world of Jane Austen. They are usually quite small and dainty, made in two simple moulds, and although having a finish almost like porcelain, they still seem to retain the true quality of earthenware. The colours are restrained and delicately harmonized, conspicuous among them being a fine dark brown and a good turquoise. The costumes of the characters have lively sprig patterns, and they usually stand upon elaborate moulded bases finished with a coloured line, generally red. Groups like the set of the Four Seasons in the Fitzwilliam Museum, if not original, show a subtle and entirely legitimate translation of Wood themes, which were themselves based on porcelain.

Bust of Jean-Jacques Rousseau. In enamel colours, probably by Enoch Wood c. 1790. 6¼ ins. high. (Victoria & Albert Museum.)

33

For one brief moment before plunging into the quite different styles and sentiments of the nineteenth century it is worth pausing and looking at one small class of figures in which one almost feels the authentic touch of those 'primitives' who made the comic little figures of the Astbury and Astbury-Whieldon days.

In material they are mostly to be found among the 'Prattwares' already mentioned, wherein high-temperature underglaze colours give an orchestra of loud and sometimes virulent browns, oranges, and hot yellows, colours which seem to have strong affinities with peasant art as seen on the Continent. Many of them were made (and marked) by Felix Pratt of Fenton, but he was by no means the only maker of them. Nor do they all have the magic touch of which I have spoken.

Most typical, perhaps, is the famous 'Umbrella Courtship' in the collection of Captain E. Bruce George, showing a charmingly comic couple all dressed in their best 'walking out' in the rain. There is a later Salt version of this called 'Dandies' but it is not at all in the same spirit. Then in the Victoria and Albert Museum (see page 29) there is a pair of ladies with puffed sleeves and spotted gowns who must be the granddaughters of the ladies sitting in the settles. A woman dressed as Ceres, in the collection of Mrs. Naginton, has the flavour too. There is comedy, grotesquery, and crudery to come in later days, but nowhere again is there quite this touch of gentle caricature.

3. The School of Walton

China fanciers will have often seen small, gaily colourful earthenware groups ornamented with amusingly simplified trees and bushes. Those who know their way around the porcelains of the 1760s and onwards will recognize them as a kind of cottage version of the rococo bocages, much used in porcelain, particularly at Chelsea, and afterwards at Derby.

They are the outstanding feature of a school of figure makers working in the last decade or two of the eighteenth century and the first two or three of the nineteenth, who are usually grouped under the names of the best known of them, John Walton of Burslem and Ralph Salt of Hanley.

One says 'best known', but in fact very little is known personally about either of these men. John Walton may or may not be the person of that name who was born to Richard and Sarah Walton at Burslem in 1780: otherwise our only information about him comes from directories. In 1818 he

A pair of sheep by John Walton. The one in reverse shows his mark. (John Hall.)

was described as a 'colour maker and earthenware manufacturer' and from 1822 to 1835 was listed as a maker of toys, figures, and Egyptian black at Navigation Road, Burslem. It now seems to be accepted that he started up on his own somewhere between 1802 and 1810, having probably worked for one of the other 'toy makers' in his youth.

Nobody will look for originality of subject in Walton's figures: on the other hand, in translating the porcelains of Chelsea–Derby (and *their* earlier models from the Continent) into simpler and more cheaply priced ornaments for the mantelpieces of the farmhouse, the cottage, and the little terrace houses springing up in the towns, Walton managed to achieve something of an original creation of his own.

These shepherds and shepherdesses, boys and girls, gardeners, huntsmen, fishwomen, and the many figures from biblical scenes, may be crudely modelled by comparison with those in porcelain, or those made by the Woods, and many have pointed to them as the 'decadence' of English figure making. But this, I think, is to miss their point: they were not—as is often done in the sometimes tasteless work of Enoch Wood—intended to imitate the originals but to translate them into another medium for a wider public. This was the world of the 'image man', pedlars with their trays of 'image toys' on their heads, who travelled the countryside and worked the streets of the towns crying their wares—offering 'Elijah and the Raven' or 'The Flight from Egypt' based on the same subjects as the crudely colourful prints which hung upon the cottage walls.

Walton's figures—except for these unmarked ones which are thought to be his early work—are invariably painted in overglaze enamels. Sometimes the same stock figures are used in different ways; for example, in the famous 'Tithe Pig' group—where a couple are offering a horrified parson their tenth child instead of their tenth pig in the litter. The same figures also appear on their own, or in other groups. He secured some very pleasingly dappled effects in his painting, and his colours are always bright. The 'tree' or

36

bush which stands beside the figure or group, consists of a cluster of foliage rather like an oak leaf, and in the centre there is a flower variously shaped and coloured either pink, dark blue, yellow, or white.

He marked his wares with his name in capitals, usually inside a cartouche at the back of the piece, for, being intended for the chimney piece, backs didn't matter. Quite often, however, the front would bear a title of some sort, such as 'Sportsman', 'Gardeners', or 'Fire', signifying one of a set of the Elements.

RALPH SALT

Bocages were also a feature of the output of Ralph Salt, who worked first at Miles Bank, Hanley, from 1812 to 1834, then at Marsh Street until his death in 1846. He made

ordinary wares, and also a very large quantity of chimney ornaments of all kinds, sometimes marking them with his name in capitals.

Salt figures, although intended for the same market as Walton's, were not slavish imitations of them. Ralph Salt turned out quite distinctive models, and there is often a humorous touch about them, especially with his animals.

His name is often found on the sheep figures, or groups of ram, ewe, and a very tiny lamb, where the clay has been roughened up to show a fine

Shepherdess by Ralph Salt, about 1820. Marked 'SALT'.

37

(Left) '*Who shall ware the breeches?*'
(Opposite) '*Polito's Menagerie*'.
*12½ ins. high. Perhaps by Obadiah
and Martha Sherratt, c. 1820/35.*

growth of wool. Salt was also
given to using metallic lustres,
and sometimes impressed the
title of the piece on the
front.

Many other potters of the
'Walton' school are known to
us only by their names on a
few pieces and an entry in a
directory. John and Ralph
Hall, of Tunstall and Burslem, put their surname in
capitals on a few pieces which
have survived. John Dale of Burslem does not appear in the
records, but his name is on two 'Element' figures in the
Victoria and Albert Museum. Charles Tittensor of Shelton
made some figures with bocages between 1815 and 1825
and seems to have harked back to the days of Wood and
Neale, for he used some attractive colours, sometimes with
a translucent green on the base.

OBADIAH AND MARTHA SHERRATT

A much more earthy and rumbustious note is to be found
in the work of Obadiah and Martha Sherratt of Hot Lane,
Burslem. Here the prettiness of little boys and girls, the
tender fun of the little Prattware figures, the gentle piety of
the religious subjects, gives place to the England of bull-
baiting, the circus, tiger-hunting, horrific murders, and the
broad comedy of domestic life—which was to find another
expression in the early Victorian farce.

Obadiah himself was born about 1796 and married as his
second wife a widow named Martha Austin—from the

marriage register it appears that neither of them could write. In the early 1820s he was making toys and figures in Hot Lane, and afterwards in Waterloo Road: he was long survived by his wife, who seems to have run the business in collaboration with their son Hamlet, after Obadiah's death.

Both Obadiah and Martha celebrated their first marriages at Norton-in-the-Moors, a kind of Gretna Green of the Potteries; and it may well be that the famous group in the Fitzwilliam Museum at Cambridge, showing a runaway marriage, refers to the Gretna of Staffordshire rather than that of the Border.

The Sherratts did not mark their pieces, but it is generally accepted that the groups, sometimes large and elaborate,

'Alebench' with the lady taking her husband by the nose to baste him: and (opposite) *'Teetotal', domestic bliss restored except that the husband still seems to have a sore head. Perhaps by Martha and Obadiah Sherratt. Early nineteenth century.*

mounted on bracket feet, are from their factory. Outstanding among these are the bull-baiting groups. These were not the first efforts to commemorate this sport, but they are among the most lively and dramatic. In one group, an example of which is to be seen in the Stoke-on-Trent Museum, a huge bull has tossed one dog on to its back and has its head lowered to gore another, while a man beside them lifts his arms and shouts at the crowd. Two oval cartouches at the side bear the words 'Bull Baiting' and 'Now Captin Lad'.

On similar-footed stands or plinths are such groups as 'Romulus and Remus', 'The Roran Lion', 'The Grecian

Slave' (see colour plate), and one especially horrific one called 'The Death of Monrow'. This depicts the unfortunate end of an officer in the Indian Army, a certain Lieutenant (not General as often given) Monro, son of Sir Hector Monro. While on a hunting trip on an Indian island, Monro was set upon by a tiger and carried off into the jungle by his head. Astonishingly, he survived long enough to stagger back into the camp with his head crushed in and with frightful lacerations, but he died a few hours later. This incident was reported in detail in a letter to the *Gentlemen's Magazine* for 1793, and it must have made a profound impression on the public to have inspired so many groups.

Perhaps the most elaborate of the groups attributed to the Sherratts is 'Polito's Menagerie', which stands a foot high and shows the entrance to this famous travelling show, which was touring England in the early years of the nineteenth century. Monkeys, lions, and tigers appear on the elaborate facia while on the platform stand the musicians, their hurdy-gurdies and pipes and drums encouraging the people to roll up and inspect the animals. After Polito's

death, the same model did duty for 'Wombwell's Circus'. One of these models was sold at Sotheby's not long ago for no less than £500.

'The Murder in the Red Barn', featuring William Corder and Maria Martin, another event which caught the imagination of the day, is the subject of another of these groups. Among scriptural subjects there is a naïve group showing Abraham about to sacrifice Isaac, which is inscribed 'Abraham Stop'.

The long line of Victorian pottery groups poking fun at domestic couples seems to have started at about this time, for some of the Sherratt type groups deal with them. There is the one where a couple are having a vigorous tussle, accompanied by labels reading 'Who shall ware the breeches' and 'Conquer or Die'. Others show first the wife threatening the husband for drinking ('The Alebench'), then a second scene, which has miraculously sprouted foliage, showing the couple sitting quietly at tea, the wife smiling happily, the husband desperate with boredom. Enormous fun must have been provided for everyone but those who received these little things; perhaps they took the first opportunity they could of passing them on to another couple.

VICTORIANA

In the days of Astbury, Whieldon, and the young Ralph Wood I, Staffordshire figures were true earthenware. Their shapes and decorations arose naturally out of the clays the potters were using for household wares: and they expressed the native genius in an entirely local way. There seems to be nothing whatever like them in any other country.

Then came porcelain with its own peculiar merits. The figures which appeared in it expressed something quite different from the homely sentiment and fun of the Staffordshire villages. It was aimed at the sophisticated luxury world of the courts and the palace, the town house and the great mansion. It embodied the extravagance and caprice of the

42

rococo in the most skilful way—as it was admirably fitted to do.

But whenever the potters tried to offer in earthenware a cheaper substitute for porcelain, they ran the danger of producing a lifeless imitation of the real thing. All through the work of the later Ralph Wood, Enoch Wood, and their successors, there was a gradual move away from the native tradition, and consequently a sad falling off in interest and quality.

Somewhere about the beginning of the Victorian era there was a change of spirit. The enormously increased demand for ornaments from an expanding population with increased spending power set up a need for something cheaper, and therefore simpler to make, less sophisticated than the imitations of porcelain—who among this new public had ever heard of Apollo or Ceres?

All these factors combined to produce a new and vigorous kind of folk art—except that it had a strong flavour of the new urban populations rather than the peasant countryside. The Victorian chimney ornament, and especially the 'flatback' as it was called, brought us back to the true world of pottery—and also to a whole world of interesting collecting which is still accessible to the modestly endowed.

CHRONICLING THE TIMES

These flatbacks—and also the 'all-round' figures in the same idiom—are truly the abstract and brief chronicle of their time. Among the portrait figures you will find the whole galaxy of royalty, soldiers, sailors, explorers, standing side by side with cricketers, actors, murderers, authors, singers, and poetesses. These ornaments reflect the political crisis of the moment, the dastardly murder in the lonely country farmhouse, the latest assassination, the great victory in battle, the acclaim earned by a famous preacher or a singer. They also show in endless variety the English love of animals, wild and tame, and the interest in country sports of a people who, though becoming industrialized, had left their hearts in the villages and lanes of their ancestors.

43

4. Royalty First

In High Victorian England, as one might expect, the royal family forms the largest single group of the portrait figures. These were the days when a demure young Queen, married to a handsome fairy-tale prince, was busy wiping out the memory of the unpleasant Hanoverians and setting that standard of simple domesticity so much needed at that time.

The Queen herself, of course, is the favourite figure and appears at every stage in her life, from Coronation to Diamond Jubilee. She appears with her children, with foreign royalty like Napoleon III, the King of Sardinia, the Sultan of Turkey—mostly to commemorate the Triple Alliance in the Crimean War. The Prince Consort is usually one of a pair with the Queen, but he is also found in his own right, sometimes alone or with allied rulers, sometimes at the hunt or with his children. These latter also were very popular, both in their youth and as they grew up, married and took their part in the national life.

The flatbacks were still about when King Edward VII succeeded to the throne, also when the late Queen Mary

(Left) *Queen Victoria and Prince Albert, with their first child, afterwards Prince of Wales and later King Edward VII.* (John Hall.) (Opposite) *Queen Victoria's first two children, with pony cart.* (John Hall.)

was betrothed to the Duke of Clarence—they appear as a pair. But there seems to be no record of George V, who ultimately married her.

STATESMEN, SOLDIERS, AND SAILORS

Among the statesmen, the Duke of Wellington seems to have been the most popular. His portraiture in pottery goes back even before the days of the flatback, for there is a story that Obadiah Sherratt used the same model for the Iron Duke's nose as for the teats on his cow milk-jugs. One group shows the victor of Waterloo mounted, with a telescope, and the inscription 'Up Guards and at Them'. A late one, evidently made after his funeral, is dedicated to his memory; another shows him in the high-backed chair in which he died at Walmer Castle.

Prime Ministers include Sir Rober Peel, Disraeli (Lord Beaconsfield), and Gladstone—sometimes as a pair with Disraeli, at other times paired off with Mrs Gladstone. Philanthropists like the Earl of Shaftesbury, patriots like Daniel O'Connell, Charles Stewart Parnell, and Louis Kossuth were also celebrated in the Staffordshire gallery.

The themes of some of the naval and military figures go back to pre-Victorian times, and no doubt were based on earlier figures, for example, Nelson, Napoleon I, Captain Cook. But in general the figures were produced by the events of the times. The Afghan War of 1842 and Sir John Franklin's expedition of 1845 seem the earliest, followed by the Crimean War, which was an extremely rich source of figures. The allied rulers, as mentioned above, lead the van, followed by the sailors and soldiers like Sir

(Above left) *Prince Alfred, Duke of Edinburgh, second son of Queen Victoria.*
(Below left) *James Rush, the Norfolk murderer.*
(Above centre) *Louis Kossuth, the Hungarian patriot who led the revolt against Austria.*
(Above right) *King Charles I.* (All John Hall.)

James Dundas, Sir Charles Napier, Lord Raglan (of the Charge of the Light Brigade), Sir George Brown, Sir James Simpson, Sir George Cathcart, Sir Charles Windham, Sir William Codrington, and also a group of the French and Turkish officers. Florence Nightingale has her niche; so too have the unnamed soldiers and sailors of the kind she helped to nurse.

46

The Indian Mutiny brought out figures like General Havelock and Sir Colin Campbell. There is also one of Highland Jessie, the wife of Corporal Brown, who at the Siege of Lucknow was the first to hear the distant pipes playing 'The Campbells are coming'.

FOREIGN FIGURES

All through the Victorian age there was a lively interest in foreign personalities, and this found expression in many of the figures used. Washington and Franklin had long appeared in all kinds of Staffordshire wares: to these were now added Abraham Lincoln, John Brown, and also Americans who had become well known in various ways in this country —for example, Van Amburgh the lion tamer; Mrs. Bloomer, inventor of the garment which bears her name; Moody and Sankey, the revivalists; and others. Garibaldi's visit to England in 1864 set off a whole crop of figures in his likeness; he was sometimes paired off with 'Garibaldi's Englishman'—that Colonel Peart who was his double, and impersonated him on one occasion. Our Victorian ancestors also looked on at the Franco-Prussian war in the persons of King William I of Prussia (whose son Prince Frederick William had married our own Princess Royal), Prince Bismarck, and Count Von Moltke.

Figures like Lord Wolseley, General Gordon, and Lord Kitchener marked later campaigns, the last of them being the Boer War, with Sir Redvers Buller, Lord Roberts, Sir John French (Lord Ypres), and Sir Robert (afterwards Lord) Baden-Powell.

Young cricketers. (John Hall.)

47

Leaders of all religious denominations have their place in the gallery. There are gibes at the Roman Catholics—the 'No-Popery' agitators brought out figures of martyrs of another age like Cranmer, Latimer, and Ridley. But they also offer tribute to St. Vincent de Paul, Cardinal Manning, and at least one of the Popes. Nonconformism is represented by John Wesley; General Booth, founder of the Salvation Army; Charles Spurgeon, the Baptist preacher, whose congregations outgrew his halls; and William Penn, founder of Pennsylvania.

Authors are led by Shakespeare and include also Milton, Voltaire, Burns (paired with his 'Highland Mary'), Byron (with his 'Maid of Athens'), Sir Walter Scott and Eliza Cook the poetess. Harriet Beecher Stowe is represented by some of the characters from *Uncle Tom's Cabin*, including Uncle Tom himself, Aunt Chloe, Eva with both Uncle Tom and Topsy, and George and Eliza Harris.

The Whirligig of Politics. In the centre, General Sir George Brown, second-in-command to Lord Raglan, is fighting alongside the French at the Crimea. Ten years later, however, the two British lions are squatting on Napoleon III during the Anglo-French war scare of 1860. The mounted figure is one of those which Mr. Balston attributes to a particular but as yet unnamed Staffordshire factory. (All John Hall.)

The Red Barn, the murderer, and his victim. (Collection: Jack Hawkins, C.B.E.)

STAGE HISTORY

Collectors interested in the history of the theatre could, with patience and—even at today's prices—with a reasonable expectation of appreciating investment, gather together a group of famous figures of the stage. Point has been given to this lately by the appearance of fine models of contemporaries like Sir Laurence Olivier.

James Quin, active in the reign of the first two Georges, appears most famously as Falstaff, not only in complete figures but also as a Toby jug. David Garrick is most often seen as Richard III, and John Kemble as Hamlet. William Macready, who dominated the stage from about 1820 to 1850, appears as Shylock and Macbeth.

In pre-Gilbert and Sullivan days, grand opera held public attention more firmly than afterwards, and one of the chief favourites with the public was Jenny Lind, the Swedish soprano, who first won all hearers in this country as Alice in Meyerbeer's *Robert le Diable*, and as Maria in Donizetti's

49

La Fille du Régiment. But she is also seen as she appeared at her many successful concerts in this country.

Sometimes long-forgotten originals are revealed by these figures. Until reading Mr. Balston's catalogues (see page 61) I had not known, for example, that the famous Dundreary whiskers were first made fashionable by the actor Edward Askew Sothern, playing a kind of Wodehouse peer in Tom Taylor's play *Our American Cousin*; he appears in a figure taken from the same photograph that was used for the front page of the sheet music of a song from the play.

SPORTSMEN

Victorian England was a great age for sport, and as might be expected, cricketers come high on the list, followed by 'pugilists', jockeys, and, of course, the huntsmen who go back to the dim beginnings of Staffordshire pottery.

Most famous of the boxers was Tom Sayers, champion of England. In one group he is teamed up with John Carmel Heenan (the 'Benicia Boy'), America's idol, a much bigger man. This fight was a national sensation, being stopped by the police after thirty-seven rounds of punishment for the courageous but outmatched Sayers. Tom Cribb and Benjamin Caunt are other boxers represented in figures.

Another famous sporting event, the cricket match between Kent and All England in 1843, is marked by the figures of Thomas Box of Sussex, the outstanding wicket-keeper of his day, and Fuller Pilch of Kent, who was considered to be England's best bat. Engravings of these two appeared in the *Illustrated London News*. Lillywhite, the celebrated bowler, appears, and later figures of cricketers have been tentatively identified with two famous members of the All England XI, George Parr and Julius Caesar.

MURDERERS GALORE

Then, as now, crime was the favourite item of news, and the celebrated murders of the day were reported in figures and groups. Highwaymen like Dick Turpin, paired with

Tom King, the associate he accidentally shot, appear early, also Will Watch, the privateer and smuggler. Murderers are headed by James Rush, owner of Potash Farm near Wymondham, which was mortgaged to the owner of nearby Stanfield Hall. Rush shot both him and his son dead and wounded two women, for which he was hanged at Norwich in 1849. This event was marked not only by the figure of Rush, but also by that of Emily Sandford, the governess he seduced, and who gave evidence against him; there are also representations of both Potash Farm and Stanfield Hall.

In the same way, both the person and the house are seen of William Palmer, the Rugeley surgeon who poisoned his wife, brother, and other persons. Among the lesser criminals are Arthur Orton, the 'Tichborne Claimant', who tried to pass himself off as the heir to the Tichborne baronetcy and fortune: after a trial lasting 188 days, he was sentenced to fourteen years' penal servitude.

The Red Barn murder already mentioned was another sensational crime which horrified the public into buying figures and groups. William Corder the murderer, Maria Martin, his victim, and the judge appear together in one group, with the barn itself on the other. There is also the group, in Mr. Jack Hawkins' collection (see page 49), which shows the doomed girl being enticed into a Red Barn framed in Waltonesque trees.

But all kinds of interests are shown in these figures. There is Grace Darling, daughter of a lighthouse keeper, who with her father braved the storms of the Northumberland coast to rescue some people from a wrecked steamer; also that Shah of Persia who so interested the British public on a visit in 1873 as to inspire the famous music-hall song 'Have you seen the Shah?' To have a figure of him on the mantelpiece was one way of seeing him.

5. Pottery Animals

Who does not know the Staffordshire spaniel, staring out at you from the mantelpiece or the cabinet with wide, almost human eyes? These animals, of a type no longer bred, were once called 'comforters', or 'spaniel's gentles', but whether they actually bore the expressions given them by the potter is one of those problems which are to be solved by the dog breeder rather than the china fancier.

But there they are in their thousands, each with a different expression—given them in the final touch of colour put on by hand. Some are only six inches high, others are towering specimens standing a foot and a half or more. They may have a gold chain round their necks, with a locket—or is it a padlock?—and often there is a basket of flowers hanging from their mouths. Made in pairs to face each other, the spots or other marks upon them can be found in most of the colours of the potter's palette—red, gold, black, brown, grey, green. One family appears in lustre colours, the subject of another book in this series. In the same styles come the clipped poodles, their upper halves covered with rough textured granules.

But more 'doggy' in every sort of way are all the working and sporting dogs. Here the men of the potteries were catering not for the lady's lap, the basket in the boudoir, but for field and farmhouse, for the hunting and shooting of the squirearchy and the coursing for which they themselves had a tremendous passion. These Staffordshire whippets and greyhounds, sometimes carrying a killed hare in their mouths, are occasionally to be identified with actual animals, winners of some famous trophy, the name being given in relief on the plinth. The McGrath and Pretender pair commemorates the winner and runner-up respectively of the Waterloo Cup in 1871.

The coursing dogs are shown in several attitudes, either standing, sitting, or lying with crossed paws. Characteristically they are in a salmon-orange shading off to brown on the back, with the features in black. The plinth, usually oval, can have a roughened top with green tufts of grass. It may be left white, but it is often found in blue.

These whippets and greyhounds also appear in what is called 'Jackfield' ware. This term was originally applied to wares made in the Shropshire town of this name, but it stands generally for pieces in red earthenware covered with

Sportsmen: (right) *tiger-shooting,* (below left) *foxhunting,* and (below right) *pigsticking.* (All John Hall.)

(Left) *'Comforters'*.
(Opposite) *Poodles*. (John Hall.)

a shiny black glaze and usually having gilt decoration. They were made throughout the Potteries, and in fact show some of the most delicate modelling of any figures.

Among other sporting dogs there are the setters, the fox-hounds, harriers, staghounds, springers, and pointers. The spotted dalmatian, the coaching dog, is not so frequently found, but much valued when he is.

Of other domestic animals, cats appear in surprisingly small numbers; presumably the domestic taste was met by the lapdog. Mounted figures are plentiful enough, but horses on their own are not as common as one might expect in a country and at a time when it was the principal means of travel, sport, and commerce, and there seems to have been little interest in showing the different breeds. Sheep were popular, from the days of the Walton ewes and lambs. From the later days one sees most often the small recumbent ewe, with roughened fleece, on its tiny blue plinth. Pigs seem to be rare, except as money-boxes.

The public Staffordshire served had been fascinated with wild animals ever since the days of Whieldon, when they were made in shapes which suggested that not many lions or elephants were ever seen in the Potteries. Bears, of course, were made from the earliest days down to the end of bear-baiting, and at one time they picked up a topical note in those which did not hug a dog but a tiny Napoleon. There were all kinds of lions, some fairly realistic, some heavily stylized, as though they were meant to be effigies rather than actual representations. Tigers, on the other hand, are rare except for the famous figure of poor Lieutenant Monro, mentioned on page 41.

Some of the prettiest models made in the Victorian era as in the days of Ralph Wood II, are the stags and hinds. Here the potter seems to have been able to hit off a gentle grace of outline without too much sentiment. Birds, tremendously popular with the porcelain men, and also with the earlier Staffordshire potters, now seem to appear mainly in the form of tureens.

Zebras are to be found more often than camels, and there are plenty of elephants, usually Indian ones. The most famous of them was, of course, Jumbo, hero of a music-hall song, who also appears on horse brasses. He was actually an African elephant kept at the Zoo, and to the general

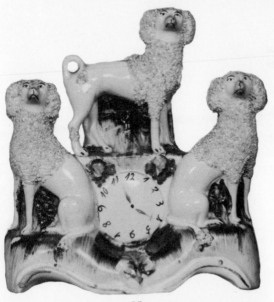

More Staffordshire Dogs. (John Hall.)

consternation of the public, was sold to Barnum, the famous circus proprietor. As always when the foundations of English life are shaken, questions were asked in the House of Commons, and much public sympathy was extended to the mate he left behind him. A popular song ran:

Jumbo said to Alice, 'I love you.'
Alice said to Jumbo, 'I don't believe you do.
If you really loved me as you said you do,
You would not go to Yankee Land and leave me
    in the Zoo.'

Jumbo, it seems, was rather difficult to control, and eventually ran into an American railway train.

Staffordshire bird in colours, observed (below) by a Staffordshire cat in black 'Jackfield' glaze over red earthenware. (John Hall.)

6. Making the Flatback

Many of these figures were being reproduced until recently, often from the original moulds, and since some of them appear without modern marks to warn the embryo collector, it may be useful to have a few facts about their production.

The flatbacks were made from moulds, in either two or three parts. There were several processes before the final figure was achieved. First an original model was made by the designer in oily clay, and from this master moulds in either two or three parts were obtained in plaster of paris. Taken off the model and reassembled, these moulds were used to create a hollow figure into which plaster of paris was poured: this provided what was called the 'block' which could now be used as an original. From the master mould—which was also kept for future use—working moulds were made, with which to turn out the figures in their hundreds. If an 'edition' sold well new working moulds could be made from the master mould.

Then followed a tidying-up process whereby the 're-pairer' scraped away seam marks, smoothed out or filled in imperfections, added extra parts where necessary, and roughened up (for sheep's wool, grass, etc.). After a few other operations the figure was fired in the oven to a 'biscuit' state, the underglaze colours—for instance the well-known blue and black—painted on, and then fired again to harden. After being dipped in a liquid lead glaze to make the piece non-porous, it was fired again, and then painted with the overglaze enamels.

It will be seen that with all these processes and the quite considerable amount of handwork which went into seem-ingly mass-produced articles, there must be considerable differences in models, even when they are taken from the same moulds. Colours can vary, parts can be blunted as the

Staffordshire animals in variety. (John Hall.)

mould gets worn, and there are generally slight variations in the 'repairing' work.

Some of the points to watch in distinguishing genuine nineteenth-century figures from modern versions arise out of these processes. For example, glazes then were not so perfect as they are today; and because of the way body and glaze contracted unevenly in the kiln, the early pieces tend to show a fine crazing which is seldom present in the modern pieces. The modern maker has also found it difficult to match the relatively impure metallic oxide colourings of the originals, and comparison with genuine pieces will generally reveal these differences quite clearly.

One of the principal makers of figures was Sampson Smith, whose marks sometimes appear on figures, and the firm which succeeded him reissued some of the figures early in the present century. These moulds were bought by a collector and distributed. Another firm surviving from the early days was using old moulds down to the year 1962.

All the while the flatbacks were being produced, however, there were many 'all around' figures. These were usually made in the traditional way by casting, i.e. by pouring clay 'slip' into a plaster of paris mould, whereupon the mould absorbed the water from the clay, leaving a layer of slip attached to the sides of the mould which could be detached to form a whole hollow figure.

In his fine study *Staffordshire Portrait Figures of the Victorian Age*—essential for anyone interested not only in this specialist field, but also in all Victorian figure making—Mr. Thomas Balston has sorted out two distinctive types, seemingly made at particular but so far unknown places. He calls one the 'Alpha' factory, featuring figures contemporary with the years 1845 to 1851. Some of them are quite complicated in design, needing as many as eight moulds. Others are in a fine porcellainous material so well modelled and painted as to be taken sometimes for Rockingham china.

Mr. Balston calls his other factory the 'Tallis', because the figures are based on engravings in Tallis's *Shakespeare*

Gallery, published in 1852–3. They are in an exceptionally hard and heavy body, and like the 'Alpha' pieces are obviously in the porcelain tradition.

He also offers indications of the existence of other types, as yet untraced to their sources. Discovering these, and putting a name to the still unidentified figures which turn up from time to time, will keep collectors of the future busy for many a long day.

BRONX N Y HULL

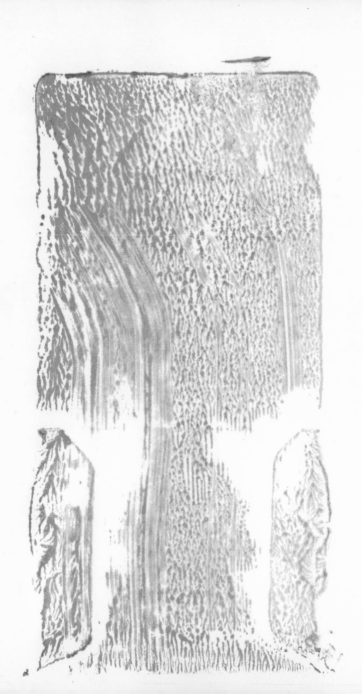